# ONE WEEK LOAN

SUE KNIGHT

**Sue Knight** is founder of The Sue Knight Partnership Ltd, an international consultancy delivering tailor-made, in-company programmes on leadership, teamwork, and personal and organisational development. The Sue Knight Partnership also offers public courses leading to recognised business certification in NLP as well as specific courses in coaching, sales and communications, and systemic enterprising for chief executives. Sue is the author of a number of books on NLP, regularly contributes articles to many business journals, and gives talks internationally on her work. She is based in Buckinghamshire but spends a large part of the year in France, where she does most of her writing. She is committed to supporting leaders to live out values of integrity, trust, respect, learning, innovation, truth and fun.

**Management Shapers** is a comprehensive series covering all the crucial management skill areas. Each book includes the key issues, helpful starting points and practical advice in a concise and lively style. Together, they form an accessible library reflecting current best practice – ideal for study or quick reference.

The Chartered Institute of Personnel and Development is the leading publisher of books and reports for personnel and training professionals, students, and all those concerned with the effective management and development of people at work. For full details of all our titles, please contact the Publishing Department:

*tel.* 020-8263 3387

*fax* 020-8263 3850

*e-mail* publish@cipd.co.uk

The catalogue of all CIPD titles can be viewed on the CIPD website:

www.cipd.co.uk/publications

# introducing
# NLP

SUE KNIGHT

CHARTERED INSTITUTE OF PERSONNEL AND DEVELOPMENT

Design by Curve
Typesetting by Paperweight
Printed in Great Britain by
The Guernsey Press, Channel Islands

*British Library Cataloguing in Publication Data*
A catalogue record for this book is available from the
British Library

ISBN
0-85292-772-X

Chartered Institute of Personnel and Development, CIPD House,
Camp Road, London SW19 4UX
Tel.: 020 8971 9000   Fax: 020 8263 3333
E-mail: cipd@cipd.co.uk   Website: www.cipd.co.uk
Incorporated by Royal Charter. Registered charity no. 1079797

# contents

## Other titles in the series:

# introduction

In the last few years a new name has crept into our business vocabulary: Neuro Linguistic Programming, or NLP for short. What a name – but, more importantly, just what is NLP, and how can it help you in your work and in your life?

I have written this book to begin to answer that question. I emphasise the word 'begin' because NLP is an enormous topic that would take a library of books to explain. And that is the point – a book can only give you an introduction to NLP. Ultimately it will be your training and practice in NLP that will demonstrate for you the true potential of this powerful tool. It is a practical, experiential means of releasing your true potential and helping you to help others do the same.

There are many, many applications of NLP in business today. Its use has blossomed in the last two to three years. I have chosen a few of the most popular areas of application – the ones that I believe can most quickly and easily make a difference to how you manage yourself, your business and your life.

It is likely that you are already using some of these ideas. What I hope is that the content of this book will make you much more aware of your true talent. We take for granted so much more aware of your true talent. We take for granted so much of what we do, and so one of my aims in the work that I do with NLP is to make the unconscious – the talents that we take for granted – conscious.

There is so much more to be learned about each of the topics covered in the following chapters and in NLP as a whole. Reading this book will be, I hope, like dipping your finger into the sauce to get a flavour of the meal that is to come. May your appetite be whetted!

# 1 what is NLP?

Consider for a moment the things that you have done well today. Maybe there are even some things that you or others around you would say that you do with excellence.

Which of these things have you done well today?

1  Woken up on time.

2  Left someone you work with in a good frame of mind after speaking to you.

3  Explained something to someone else in a way that he or she understood.

4  Moved a bit further forwards in achieving your goals, or even totally achieved some.

5  Successfully handled a telephone call.

6  Inspired someone to do something he or she has not done before.

7  Given feedback in a way that was received positively.

8  Learned something unexpectedly.

9  Successfully negotiated a potential conflict either at work or at home.

10 Made a new acquaintance with whom you look forward to having future contact.

All of them? Some of them? None? Whatever your answer is, you have a strategy for achieving whatever it was that you did (and do) achieve. If, for example, you succeeded in inspiring someone to do something that he or she has not done before, you have a strategy for doing this. The chances are that you are aware of some of the elements of your strategies but, equally, the chances are that there are some crucial bits of which you have no conscious knowledge. Most of us take for granted the fact that every day we do some things well.

Now answer the same question for these things: which of these have you done 'well' today?

1 Become upset or stressed.

2 Given up on a goal.

3 Missed a deadline.

4 Left someone feeling frustrated with you.

5 Felt frustrated with yourself.

6 Got into an argument.

7 Damaged a friendship.

8 Attempted to influence someone but succeeded only in arousing his or her resistance to change.

9   Said something that you did not mean to say and now regret.

10  Slammed the phone down.

It may seem strange to ask whether you did any of these things 'well' but, whatever you did, underlying your behaviour there is a strategy for achieving exactly the result that you did achieve.

For example, people who are skilled at influencing others usually do some or all of the following:

● Get themselves in the best possible emotional and mental state.

■ Believe that they can get their point of view across in a way that invites the attention of those around them.

▲ Talk to themselves in an encouraging and positive internal voice.

◉ Match subtly the other person's body language in a respectful way.

● Sense the kind of words that the other person is using in his or her conversation.

● Use the same kind of words in response.

■ Read the signals that tell them when they have achieved rapport.

▲ Identify what is important to the other person in the way that he or she makes decisions.

● Recognise when they have a strong enough connection with the other person to take a lead in the conversation in a way that he or she will accept.

In each case, a strategy is at work: a sequence of thinking and behaviour patterns driven by beliefs and values that gets a result. NLP is a means of eliciting these strategies both from ourselves and from other people. But teams and companies have strategies, too. So if we want to know how we or someone else – or indeed a team or company – achieves results, then with NLP we have the tools to find out. This process is known as *modelling*. So, NLP is a process of *modelling* what works (the conscious and especially the unconscious processes) in order that we can reproduce the same results for ourselves. Additionally, we can teach the strategy to other people so that they can consistently reproduce the desired result.

### The name

'The name' refers to the elements that make up this process of modelling: *neuro*, *linguistic* and *programming*.

**Neuro**     This refers to the thinking patterns that make up the mental aspect of our strategies. We take information in and hold it in our minds in *visual*, *auditory* and *kinaesthetic* (feeling) ways. For example, part of a strategy to feel confident at the start of giving a presentation might be to *see* ourselves as though in a full-colour movie doing the presentation in the way that we would ideally like to do it. We might *hear* an encouraging internal voice urging us to do well. We might imagine both the smooth *feel* of the table beside us as we stand, and also the steady, confident feeling in our stomach as we begin to speak.

**Linguistic**      The second element in NLP refers to the way we use language both inwardly to ourselves (our 'inner dialogue') and outwardly in conversation with others. With NLP, we can become aware of the patterns in our own and others' language and, likewise, the effect of these patterns on both ourselves and others. For example, did you realise that if you ask people 'Why not?' when they say they cannot do something that you have influenced them to become even more resistant to the idea of doing it? A more effective question may be 'What would happen if you did do this?'

**Programming**      The programmes that we run are our strategies for getting results in all areas of life and work. Sometimes those results are what we want; at other times they do not seem to meet any conscious need. We are like computers, in that we have codes (mental and behavioural, in our case) for running our lives. Sometimes those codes work well; at others they have 'bugs' and so, instead of achieving the results we want, we sabotage our seemingly desired success. Sometimes we have the right code but use it inappropriately. For example, you might be perceived as stubborn in the way that you hang on to a point of view when it would be better to let go. What you could do, however, is use that same code to hold on tenaciously to your goals when faced with disappointment. Stubbornness can become tenacity when used appropriately. NLP is a means of tapping into the wealth of resources that we all have within to support ourselves in achieving what we really want.

The name 'Neuro Linguistic Programming' originated in California. It was developed in 1975 by Richard Bandler and John Grinder; their interest lay in how they could reproduce the excellence of people whose performance they admired.

## The applications

The applications of NLP are many and grow day by day. That, for me, is the beauty of NLP: it is an evolving subject that continually opens doors to further learning.

Some of the most popular applications of NLP in business are to:

- learn how to build and enhance relationships with new and existing contacts in such a way that you can understand and appreciate each person's point of view and, in so doing, build the rapport with which to do effective business

- develop the skills of self-management that enable you to 'keep your head' when the world around you is reeling

- learn how to recognise natural talents within yourself and others, and be able to select and draw on the skills that you require in order to achieve the results you want

- learn how to make changes stick

- find out what you really want, and develop the rapport with yourself to achieve it

- build the skills of mentoring, so that those who are being mentored have the modelling skills to be able to get the most from their mentors

- develop the coaching skills needed for you to be able to appraise your staff's performance in ways that lead to learning for you, the jobholder and the company

- enhance your ability to inspire and motivate those around you with your sense of direction and your capacity to communicate in ways that are compelling

- develop the consultancy skills needed to facilitate change

- encourage accountability, so that you and others take

ownership of your experience and your contribution to business and to life.

## What you think is what you get

NLP works on the principle that although you cannot change the world you can change the way in which you represent the world in your thinking.

Consider for a moment where you have chosen to focus your attention today. Has your attention been on:

- recent successes
- problems that you have or expect to have
- what is happening around you
- the marvels of life
- what others have said to you
- what you truly want for yourself and your family?

What is the effect of your choice of things to think about? Are you feeling good about yourself, or are you feeling down? The choice is yours.

By choosing where to focus your attention, you influence your perception of the world at large. You have only to think of the glass as half full rather than half empty to shift your state, your emotions and your pleasure in life significantly.

This pleasure ripples out. If you take pleasure in life, people around you take pleasure in your company. Those people are more likely then to choose to do business with you and to want you as a colleague, a friend and a partner.

Think of some results that you would like to achieve in your work, with your family, in your life in general. Write them down on a sheet of paper. What resources do you have within yourself that you can draw on to achieve these goals? Write these down as well.

### Case-study

Joe and Alan were colleagues on the management team. Invariably they disagreed with each other in meetings, no matter what the topic. Joe got increasingly stressed by Alan's responses to any idea that he (Joe) put forward. Whenever there was a meeting planned, Joe found himself worrying about the likely response from Alan and the expected battle of wills. Even when Alan was on holiday, Joe would talk about how difficult it would have been if Alan had been present. Not only that, but Joe always chose to anticipate unproductive meetings. Joe 'took Alan with him' in his thinking wherever he went (in his head!). But once Joe became aware of this, he began to make some different choices as to where he directed his attention. And would you believe it – the relationship between Joe and Alan began to improve!

## And finally...

What you think is what you get.

# 2 getting through

I can see what you are saying but I can't picture what it is that you want me to do. When I look back on some of the decisions that we have made in these meetings in the past, I'm just not clear what it is that we have achieved. It's all very well trying to paint a picture of our successes, but you don't seem to be giving any thought to what has been left undone. I don't want to rock the boat, but I don't think that things are at all the way you have depicted them. You may be excited about what you have proposed, but I'm just left feeling frustrated.

Now suppose that you want to influence this person. Do you know what choices you need to make in the way that you respond to him? He is 'telling' you what style works for him by the way that he is communicating with you. What you need to do is to listen not only to what he says but also to the way in which he says it.

This person is telling you that he:

- needs to 'see' an idea to understand it

- ■ thinks more naturally about the past than the future

- ▲ pays attention to what is missing rather than to what is present

- ◖ is influenced by external events more than by his own internal desires.

Suppose that you were to seek to give assurance by telling him what your proposal would do for him in the future? The chances are that he would feel even more frustrated. So what can you do?

## Connecting with other people

Anyone who needs to achieve results through others needs to be able to connect with people, no matter what their background, style or culture. Princess Diana had this skill: she was able to connect with people in all walks of life and at all levels of community and business. It is a rare skill. Those who have it engender respect and trust. This is what constitutes *rapport*.

People like people who are like themselves. We seek out people to whom we can relate. We usually recognise these people unconsciously and may relate to any of the following areas:

- ◉ our choice of leisure interests

- the kind of people we are
- what we hold to be important
- our purpose in life
- the kind of surroundings we choose
- the kind of friends that we have
- our style of talking.

The more sensitive we are to these things in other people, and the more we respect them, the more likely we are to make the connection that leads to rapport. Rapport is influence.

**Rapport is a two-way street**

Those who are successful in being able to influence people and situations expect to have rapport with anyone with whom they come into contact. They have learned either intuitively or consciously to match the style of the people with whom they are dealing. But what is significant is that not only are they able to influence – they are open to influence.

## Choosing your style

Let's reconsider the case-study at the opening of this chapter. Let's highlight some of the words that are clues for the choice of style with which to respond.

I can *see* what you are saying *but I can't picture* what it is that you want me to do. When I *look back* on some of the decisions that we have made in these meetings in the *past*, I'm just *not clear* what it is that we have achieved. It is all very well trying to *paint a picture* of our successes, *but* you *don't* seem to be giving any thought to what *has been* left *undone*. I *don't want* to *rock the boat* but I *don't think* that things are at all the way you have *depicted* them. You may be *excited* about what you have proposed, *but I'm just left feeling frustrated*.

People who are skilled in building rapport would make the following choices in the way that they respond. They would:

- choose predominantly visual words in the way that they speak. For example, they might *match* some of the visual vocabulary that the other person used ('see', 'picture', 'clear', 'paint a picture'). They might add some new ones, but still using this same visual sense, eg 'Let's focus on…', 'You may begin to notice…' or 'Looking back on some of the scenarios…'.

- choose some kinaesthetic language to match such phrases and words as 'rock the boat' and 'excited'.

- start in the past to *match* the time orientation of the other person, eg 'What we have done…', 'What you were clarifying…', 'The last time we were watching out for…'.

- emphasise what was not the case rather than what was, eg 'I realise I did not point out…', 'What we didn't do was…' and 'Where we went wrong was…'.

- recognise that external events trigger feelings for this person and then reflect that in saying something like 'I can see how this must have made you feel.'

The effect of this is to acknowledge the other person for who and *how* he or she is. This gives a very powerful message to the other person's subconscious mind that he or she has been recognised.

There are many more choices that we each make in the way that we think and speak and act. These include the extent to which we pay attention to:

- what we do or do not want

- what is happening around us, or what we are feeling on the inside

- the big picture – the global situation – or the facts and details

- what is and what is not there

- what we see, hear, feel physically or emotionally, taste or smell

- the past, the present or the future

■ the people, the place, what we are doing, the time or occasion or the subject in hand.

These are a few of the choices that we make in how we direct our attention both in our thinking and in our environment. Our thoughts leak out in our choice of words. The skill is to choose words that fit with the way that others think.

Let's see how sensitive you are to the spoken word now. What does the following passage tell you about the style of the person who is speaking?

What I would really like to achieve from this meeting is a decision. To do that, I would like to suggest that we ask everyone how they feel about what I am proposing for the future of the department. I have my instincts as to what you are feeling, but I sense that it is important to talk things through before we move ahead.

Write down what you think this person's preferred ways of thinking and communicating are. Choose from the following:

● what he or she does or does not want

■ visual, auditory or kinaesthetic

▲ past, present or future.

Here are some clues:

● This person is using words that suggest she prefers feelings – words like 'feel', 'instincts', 'feeling', 'move ahead'.

■ The first sentence ('What I would really like…') is a clue as to whether her preference is for problems or a desired future state. The preference is made clearer by the following proactive statement: 'I would like to suggest…'.

▲ As for her time-orientation, the clues are to be found in such words and phrases as 'I would like to', 'the future of the department', 'move ahead'. Clearly, she is oriented towards the future.

These are a few examples of the choices in our vocabulary that signpost our unique style of thinking and communicating. There are many more.

## What to look for

I have concentrated here on the choice of words because of the restrictions imposed on me by having to communicate with you by means of the printed page. If you were able to see the people that I have used as case-studies, you would detect visual as well as verbal characteristics for each style.

Here are some examples:

## People thinking and speaking in...

| a visual way | an auditory way | a kinaesthetic way |
|---|---|---|
| look up | look to their ears | look down |
| gesture skywards | adopt a telephone posture, with hand on ear and mouth | gesture down to the floor |
| breathe high in the chest | breathe mid-chest | breathe low in the chest |

## People thinking and speaking in...

| a problem-oriented way | a desired-future-state way |
|---|---|
| show tension in their face and body | have relaxed body and facial muscles |
| frown | smile |
| hold themselves in a closed way | are expansive and open in their gestures |

## People thinking and speaking in...

| the past | the present | the future |
|---|---|---|
| look to their left | look you in the eye | look to their right or straight ahead, unfocused |

(The direction of gaze for some people may be reversed.)

Your skill lies not so much in learning what I have written here but in attending to the people in your life in such a way that you learn what is true for them. And it is important to recognise that our demeanour may differ from one context to another. This skill is *not* about labelling and 'boxing' people; it *is* about developing our sensitivity to what people are telling us, not only regarding what they say but regarding especially *how* they say it.

## And finally...

True rapport is the ability to dance in step with your partner.

# leading the way

So you have rapport. Now what? Well, rapport is enough if you just want to put yourself in the other person's shoes to find out how he or she experiences the world. However, most of us have goals to achieve and directions in which we want to move. Building rapport creates the relationship that will encourage others to want to walk with us on that journey. Yet this begs the question 'Where do you want to go?'

Sometimes the building bricks of NLP are defined as:

- establishing rapport
- creating a compelling direction
- sensitivity towards yourself and others
- flexibility to make new choices if what you are doing is not working.

Many people have ambitions. Some turn them into reality. Using NLP, we have researched just what it is that makes the difference between achieving that reality and failing to do so. By applying the discoveries that we have made, you can consistently achieve what you really want.

## Making your goals achievable

What are some of the things that you want?

Take a moment and allow yourself to know your goals. Write them down here. You may have many, a few or perhaps none at all. Your goal may be to know what you really do want.

_____

_____

_____

_____

_____

Now let's explore the characteristics of those goals that are most likely to be achieved (*well-formed outcomes*).

If your goals meet the criteria listed below, you are maximising the likelihood that you will achieve them. The criteria are drawn from people who are consistently able to achieve what they want, and provide a format that works for short-term goals just as well as it does for your life's ambitions. You can improve the likelihood that you will get what you want from a business meeting just as much as you can improve the standard of performance that you want in your leisure or sporting interests (some of the learning about well-formed outcomes originated in the world of golf!).

Take one of the goals that you have listed above and develop it against each of the following criteria:

1    Imagine what you *really* (and I do mean *really*) want.

2    Step into it, as though you have it. Put aside all thoughts of practicalities, of what is or is not realistic. What does this goal look, sound and feel like?

3    Make sure that your goal is within your control. For example, making your children successful is not within your control, but it is within it to be the kind of parent who supports his or her children in knowing what they really want. Being the managing director of the company that you work for may not be within your control. However, it is within it to develop yourself to have the skills and style that encourage others to want you to lead them.

4    Allow yourself to know how achieving this goal takes you one step nearer to achieving a much deeper, longer-term goal.

5    Ensure that the achievement of this goal is of real benefit to the key people in your work and in your life.

6    Consider what has been keeping you from achieving this goal to date, ie what the payoff has been for keeping your present state.

7    Ensure the goal is compelling. Does it make the hairs on the back of your neck stand on end?

8    Be clear whether you are willing to pay whatever price (even if you are unsure what that is) necessary to achieve this goal.

9    Decide what your first step towards achieving your plan will be. What is your level of commitment to taking it?

## Communicating your goals

In order for your goals to be compelling to others, they need to be compelling to you. Influence works from the inside out. It all starts with yourself.

Successful people not only have compelling outcomes: they also have compelling language with which to communicate those outcomes. However, you do not get one without the other. You might massage your language, but for an outcome to be compelling to others it has to feel compelling to you. If your inner world is impoverished and lacking in lustre, you can be sure that this will leak through in your language. If your inner world is rich and vibrant, however, your words will have the capacity to communicate this to the world at large.

People with influence use language that is rich in its appeal to all one's senses. They communicate their outcomes with language that enables others to see, hear, feel, touch, taste and even smell that future as if they apprehended it through all their senses. As a result, the unconscious minds of their listeners try on the desired outcome for size and, the more senses their minds try, the more those listeners believe that they actually have the outcome already. If your unconscious likes what is proposed, if it gives its approval, then 'Bingo!', you have the belief that you can achieve that goal, and you have the motivation. Even when you step out of that imagined state, you have left the doors open to the opportunities that will support your achieving what you want.

### Case-study

When the salesman sold me my current car, he created a scenario in which I imagined arriving in France after maybe eight or nine hours' driving. In my mind I was opening the car door as I pulled up on the drive to our house, and I stepped out as cool and fresh as when I started the journey the day before. In fact I was even cooler and more relaxed than when I started out. The journey had been one of comfort and ease. I could not get that image out of my mind. It had pushed all my hot buttons! Needless to say, I bought the car.

This is elegant influence. This was not some pushy salesman offering me a deal. This was someone who discovered and respected what was important to me. And, most important of all, the car not only lived up to but even surpassed the promise.

## And finally...

It is our 'thought-life' and not our circumstances that determines our success and happiness.

# 4 negotiating the journey

Our life is series of negotiations. Each day is series of negotiations. Do you win, or do you lose? Do you give up, or do you hang on in there, hoping that something or someone will change? Or do you consistently navigate the hurdles in ways that get a win for everyone involved? And I do mean a true *win* for everyone – one that meets your and the other person's *real* needs at one and the same time.

Knowing how to negotiate (and I don't mean playing the game of overstating your needs in order to fall back to your true position) creates the climate for real commitment and for finding innovative answers to problematic situations.

People who have the skill of navigating their way expertly through the conflicts that face them each day expect to have rapport with everyone with whom they come into contact. They assume it and they have it. They often get this rapport from their ability to put themselves into others' shoes and appreciate situations from others' perspectives.

This skill of appreciating situations from different perspectives can be learned with NLP. This can be particularly rewarding where there is imbalance between individuals' perspectives, as we shall see in the following case-study.

## Case-study

Bill and Peter were co-directors of a marketing company. Bill tended to be the visionary; Peter looked after the finances. When Bill had a new idea, he needed Peter to agree to the funding. Often Peter said no. Bill usually got more and more frustrated, and so he tried pushing harder by presenting his idea to Peter in ever more innovative ways. The more he pushed, the more Peter dug his heels in and resisted. The more Peter resisted, the more frustrated Bill became. Eventually, during a presentation that I was giving on negotiation, Bill worked the situation through to the point at which he realised how his constant bombardment of ideas made Peter feel threatened. Bill finally acknowledged that the solution was, as he put it, to 'shut up' and give Peter some space.

Think of any situations in your life right now where you do not see eye to eye with the other person, where you are not on the same wavelength or where you both fail to appreciate each other's position.

1    Which situations exist because you are able to see only your own point of view and are quite unable to consider the other person's situation?

2   In which situations do you feel such empathy towards the other person that you have lost the sense of what is important to you?

_____

_____

3   In which situations do you find it difficult to feel any emotion, and can only consider what is happening objectively and rationally, even though you know this is not enough to find a way forward?

_____

_____

## Appreciating situations from different positions

Most people have situations in their work and in their home lives in which they would like new choices – when what they are doing is not working as well as it might. It does not have to be a disaster for you to want new choices. In fact, it is your skill in improving what is already OK that can make the difference between good and great work.

People who are skilled in this way of thinking follow these sorts of step:

1   Think of a situation with another person that is not working out as well as you would like, or one in which you wish to have some new options.

2    Imagine the situation from your position, first of all: what it looks like, what it sounds like, and what it physically and emotionally feels like. That is all you need do, ie re-experience what it is like to be in the situation. If it helps to imagine the other person in a typical environment, then do so.

3    Shake yourself out of that state and now put yourself in the shoes of the other person. To do this, imagine that same situation as if you were seeing it through the other person's eyes, hearing it through his or her ears, and physically and emotionally feeling what it is like to be that person. You don't have to be right: you just have to allow yourself to imagine the situation as if you are that person in the way that you experience what is happening. This is a way of arriving at an answer to the question 'What has to be true for that person to be saying and doing what he or she is saying and doing?'

4    Now get out of that state, and this time take an objective stand on what is happening. The way to do this is to imagine that you are an outsider looking in on the 'you' in the situation and the other person. Imagine you are a fly on the wall seeing and hearing both people, but without the emotions. Allow yourself to begin to realise how connected these two people are. The fact that both people are doing what they are doing exacerbates a relationship that is already not working well. Of course, the only person that you can change is yourself. When you recognise what you are doing that is contributing to

the total scenario, then you can change your behaviour. This change in itself will have an influence on the whole relationship.

5   Step back into your own shoes, but now with the understanding and learning that you have gained from appreciating the situation from all these other perspectives.

This is the thinking that is most likely to lead to a win/win outcome. It is illustrated in the figure below.

*Seeing it from every perspective*

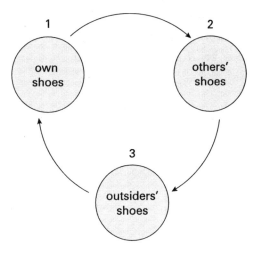

Skilled negotiators are very good at appreciating situations from their own position and, in so doing, being clear about what it is that they personally want as an outcome. However, along with this they have the ability to appreciate other people's positions, as well as being able to stand back and view the situation with detachment.

## Questions

1   What situations do you have with other people in which you would like new choices and a better way of understanding what is happening?

2   How are you making the situation what it is by either aggravating it, supporting it or encouraging it?

3   How could you change what you are doing and so lead the other person to the need for a different way of responding?

This ability to put yourself in others' shoes and, especially, to be able to see as though from the outside the dynamic of which you are a part is at the heart of systems thinking and continuous learning.

## And finally...

Fish are the last to see the water in which they swim.

# 5 making meanings that work for you

We cannot change other people – we can only change ourselves. We cannot control what happens in the world around us – we can only manage our response to it. People who lead lives of satisfaction and joy do just that: they make meaning of their life in a way that works for them whatever the circumstances.

## Case-study

One of my friends watched his son playing an important school football match. He played well but was substituted after the first half. The boy was despondent and almost inconsolable. When his father approached him, all the boy could think of was the fact that he had been taken out of play. His father started to talk to him and pointed out how well he had played in the first half, especially how he had supported the other players. Eventually the boy responded and said, 'Yes, I did, and I set up a really good goal.' His whole demeanour brightened. He had started to make a meaning that worked for him and that would probably influence his selection the next time!

## Reframing

It is our ability to frame and reframe situations in ways that work for us that is the key to how we manage our state of mind. If, for example, you take feedback as adverse criticism, you may find that you feel frustrated and even annoyed when someone makes a comment to you. If, however, you frame all feedback as learning, and if learning is important to you, then all feedback, no matter how it is given, becomes a gift.

What emotional states have you experienced so far today? Tick those that have been true for you:

- pleasure
- frustration
- curiosity
- sadness
- joy
- anger
- stress
- delight
- confidence
- indecision
- certainty
- acceptance.

What others have been true for you?

_____

_____

_____

_____

_____

To what extent have these states been ones that you would have chosen for yourself? To what extent are they ones to which you would have preferred an alternative? How you think about what happens to you is instrumental in creating your emotional state.

### Case-study

I was commenting to a friend about how much my husband had been getting on at me about completing certain tasks that we had agreed. I explained how frustrated I felt about this. My friend pointed out how much my husband must care about me to 'keep on my case' in the way that he was. Having reconsidered what he was doing in this new 'frame', I realised that I really had reason to appreciate him and not feel frustrated by what he was doing.

This is the skill of reframing. The skill is not to change what is happening but to change what we do with what is happening. Consider any moments today when you have had time to reflect on whatever is happening in your life. How did you feel when you emerged from those moments of inner dialogue and thought? The state in which you emerged tells you whether you are making meanings that work for you or not.

## Blowing the dust off your beliefs

We carry our beliefs around with us wherever we go. They are our baggage. What matters is whether they are baggage we want and need or whether they are like the extra clothing that remain in the suitcase throughout the holiday. Maybe now is the time to take those beliefs out of the suitcase and blow off the dust. In this way you can begin to decide which ones you want to keep with you because they are a support to becoming who you want to be, and which ones can be discarded because they no longer have any use.

Some of your beliefs may have been learned from parents or the equivalent of parent figures in your life. Do you believe, for example, that children should be seen and not heard, or that you should respect your elders and betters? Some beliefs may have been acquired and developed over time. Maybe you have been let down by others and now believe that you cannot trust anyone but yourself. Or maybe you believe that life always turns out well in the end.

Whatever their origin, however, beliefs are not facts. Beliefs are emotionally held opinions that we take to be true and that determine our subsequent actions. We spend our lives proving our beliefs to ourselves. If you think you are a failure, then you will set yourself up to prove this to yourself. If, though, you believe yourself to be someone who always falls on their feet, then chances are that you always will!

## Choosing beliefs that work for you

I have found there to be a core set of beliefs held by people who have the ability to manage themselves in the way that they want. You probably have some of your own beliefs that work in this way and that are unique to you. Or maybe you hold variations of the ones described below.

Try these on for size and explore what they do for you:

● *The quality of your communication lies in the effect that it achieves.*
   The kind of person who is most likely to survive and succeed in the changing world in which we live today is one who takes responsibility for the effect that he or she has on other people, their work and their lives. You are only as good as the results you achieve. A headmaster who has transformed a problem school in Yorkshire says, 'There is no such thing as bad pupils – there are only bad teachers.' An emotive statement, but a belief that has enabled him to take a hold on the way the school was being managed and transform it into one of which everyone can now be proud. People who hold the belief at the head of this paragraph do not rely on others to achieve what is important to them – nor do they blame

anyone but themselves when things do not turn out as expected. By believing that the quality of the communication lies in the effect that it achieves, they recognise that what happens is feedback on the quality of what they are doing. If, for example, such a person explains a new idea to a team of people, and that team does not like the idea, then he or she will explore what it was about the idea or the way in which it was presented that failed to achieve the desired result. He or she would not blame the members of the team for lack of intelligence or an inability to embrace new ideas.

■ *There is learning in everything that happens.*
If there is one talent that we need above all others today, it is the ability to learn. And not just to learn from courses and books, but to learn from everything that happens around us. People who can do this have the flexibility to adapt to changing circumstances. It is likely that such people will embrace uncertainty and instability as a means of learning new skills. Economic recession will hold no threat for them; they would be more likely to embrace the situation as an opportunity to learn. The capacity to learn from whatever happens stems from a belief that there is always learning available; you need only to choose to take it. These people also believe that changing circumstances offer infinite possibilities for learning and growth. If, for example, they set a course towards their vision but do not immediately achieve it, they will not give up; they will look for another way to replace the one that did not work. This willingness to

look for another way leads to flexibility and personal growth.

▲ *The map is not the territory.*
We each have our own perception of the world, and that perception is all that we have. It is not right or wrong, nor is it 'reality', but it serves a purpose just as a map does, even though it is only a representation of the territory. Each of us experiences the world through a set of filters that constitutes our perception – everyone does this. However, every individual's set of filters is unique to that person. By managing where we focus our attention, we can influence this perception and consequently influence our experience and our emotional state. We cannot manage the world, but we can increasingly manage ourselves.

● *There is a solution to every problem.*
People who succeed in achieving what they want are also those who hang on in there when the going gets rough. Because they have the belief that the goal is possible, they will suffer setbacks and come through them, learning new choices along the way. For them, the goal is a direction and a source of strength that they can hold on to when what they hoped for fails initially to materialise. These are the people who believe that there is a way forwards even if they do not know at that time exactly what the way forward is. Someone who holds this belief is more likely to find creative and innovative solutions to both old and new problems.

● *There is no failure, only feedback.*
What do you think will be your experience if you believe the above to be true for:

O moments when you do not achieve a goal on which you had set your heart?

_____

_____

_____

☐ those times you have worked really hard at something only to have someone tell you that he or she does not like what you have done?

_____

_____

_____

The core theme of all these beliefs is ownership of one's experience – a willingness to take responsibility for all that happens and to learn from it.

## Beliefs check-list

Which of the following beliefs do you hold? Tick the ones that are true for you:

1 The only person that I can absolutely change in this world is myself.

2  No one's perception of the world is any more right than that of anyone else.

3  What we think is what we get.

4  We are at the mercy of fate and circumstance.

5  We cannot change the way we are.

6  Our level of influence is determined by our ability to connect with other people.

7  If I have an idea, then it is up to other people to decide whether they want to follow it. Once I have presented it they can basically take it or leave it.

8  I have a right to ask for what I really want.

9  I can take something positive out of every situation no matter how painful or uncomfortable.

10  Goals have to be realistic, and dreaming is just a way of setting yourself up for disappointment.

Which of the ones that you have ticked support you in achieving what you really want, and which ones hinder you?

How would you really like to feel at the end of today? What can you choose to believe that will support you in achieving this?

So how come we do not always achieve what we say we want? Well, we can be skilled in sabotaging our expressed intentions.

Ways of sabotaging your success may include believing that:

- you don't have the time to do this now

- there is no point, because these are only mind games that don't really work

- you are never going to have what you really want, no matter what you do

- you are not in a position to influence what you want

- you will do it after you have...

- this will only lead to disappointment.

Ways of making your success more likely include believing that:

- it's worth a try

- who knows – this might work

- it'll be fun to find out what the result is at the end of the day

- if I don't try this out I'll never know whether it works or not

- I am (you are) worth the investment.

You are making choices like these every moment of every day. You define the quality of your life by what you do in these moments. By making meanings that work for us when we come into contact with things that create a buzz, we have the power to keep wonderfully poised in the midst of it all.

## And finally...

If you believe you can, you might. If you believe you can't, you won't.

# 6 making change stick

How often have you committed yourself to doing something, only to find that your willpower has faded by the next day? And how often have you thought you had commitment from the team around you, only to find that they too have lost the momentum when the immediacy of the moment has passed? Having the ability to make commitments stick has to be one of the most important factors in your ability to manage your time. When you have this skill you have no need to revisit your intentions: the energy to act stays with you until the act is complete.

### Case-study

Chris had offered his goal of losing weight as an example of commitment at a workshop I was running. He had turned it into a compelling outcome by realising that what would motivate him was the thought of being able to play actively with his daughter longer than he then could. We explored what would make this stick so that the next time he was faced with a tempting dessert he would still be able to say no. He created a picture of himself trampolining with his daughter; immediately he did this, his whole physiology shifted and he became quite flushed. I asked him what he needed to keep his goal alive, and he replied without hesitation that he had it – this image of the trampoline.

## Making associations that work for you

We randomly create associations in our lives all the time. We connect events to certain triggers without even realising that we are doing it. I was overwhelmed with the smell of pine as I cycled home today, and images of Christmas came immediately to mind. Maybe you have heard a tune today on the radio that reminded you of a special person.

Our senses trigger responses. In your own life there may be a:

● picture that reminds you of a special time

■ perfume that reminds you of someone dear

▲ taste that takes you back to a special meal

● certain kind of material the feel of which triggers a sense of comfort

● favourite piece of music that brings about a desired mental state.

You probably have all sorts of variation on these kinds of positive connection; some you may have set up consciously, whereas some may have just happened.

You may also have associations that have a less positive effect on you:

● the colleague who triggers feelings of apprehension in

you when you are faced with the prospect of a meeting with him

■ a situation that immediately sets off a negative inner dialogue in your head

▲ a certain tone of voice from someone close to you that stimulates immediate tension

▲ the prospect of a piece of work that conjures up negative images in your mind

● a piece of news that leads to negative 'could have been' scenarios.

## Choosing your response

How would you like to be able to access at will the positive, helpful feelings that you want? If you could do this, what feelings would you choose? Different states lend themselves to different situations. For example, I recognise that the state in which I write best is quite different from the state in which I make presentations. Equally, the state in which I can make headway with a problem is not at all the same as the state I need to finish off a piece of work on which I have been engaged for some time.

List overleaf some of the different kinds of work that you do, and name the state of mind that you would like for each one.

| Type of work | Desired state |
| --- | --- |
| (eg) writing | relaxed and introverted |
| (eg) giving a presentation | energised and extroverted |
| (eg) selling | amused and easy-going |
|  |  |
|  |  |
|  |  |

The skill of accessing the state of mind that you want whenever you choose comes from making an association – an *anchor* between a trigger and a response. You can use any sense that works for you in doing this. In the case-study I gave above, Chris used his visual sense. Often, people think of a specific example of the sense of touch; for example, you might associate a touch on your shoulder with a state of intense curiosity.

So how do you develop this skill? Here's how:

1    Choose the situation in which you would like to select your emotional state.

2    Identify a time when you have had this state before, even though that might have been in a different context or a

long time ago.

3   Step back into that time when you did have the state that you want. See it, hear it and feel it – fully immerse yourself into that time as if you were there right now.

4   Choose an anchor. It may be something quite specific that you can use as your trigger for this state – a light pinch on your earlobe, perhaps, if you want to use the sense of touch. It helps if it is also something that you can reproduce easily.

5   Step fully into the state that you want and, when it is at its maximum intensity, use your anchor, ie make the touch or the sound or the visual that you have chosen as the anchor. As soon as the state starts to fade, stop using the anchor (you want it associated with the peak desired state only). This need take just a few seconds. Do this as many times as necessary for you to feel that you have made the association.

6   Test the anchor by applying the trigger without thinking of the situation first.

## Making desirable associations for others

Have you ever wondered what sort of associations people make regarding you? Suppose one of your colleagues knows he or she is about to have a meeting with you; what sort of response do you think that triggers in your colleague? Is he or she filled with pleasure at the expectation that you will break new ground in your thinking, or filled with dread of a 'drains-up' review of all that has gone wrong? You need to know, especially if you depend on the way you are received by others to fulfil your role in business.

Now consider the following. What do you suppose would be the response on the part of a:

- member of your staff who is about to be appraised by you

- long-term customer who has dealt with you consistently over time

- colleague entering your office (area) to request something from you?

- member of your family about to tell you about something important that has gone wrong?

What would you like the response to be for these and any other everyday situations? The ability to create the appropriate reaction to key events is as important as your ability to build rapport.

*If, when you drive, you decide that you will pay attention to all the yellow cars on the road, then you can be sure that you will see a lot of yellow cars, and maybe even wonder how come you had never noticed so many before. Similarly, if you decide to be on the look-out for opportunities to enhance your key goals, then this is what you will begin to notice.*

What would you like to prime yourself to notice or to get today?

_____

_____

_____

Suppose you wanted a member of your staff to feel motivated and enthusiastic each time he or she was about to have a meeting with you. How would you manage this meeting, and as many subsequent ones as may be necessary to create that association?

_____

_____

You also need to check that you have created the appropriate anchor, ie that it works in the way that you want it to. There is a number of ways in which you could check this:

● You could ask the other person how he or she feels about the meeting.

■ You could put yourself into the other person's shoes to get a sense of how he or she might be feeling.

▲ You could calibrate your colleague's state, ie watch how he or she responds verbally and non-verbally at times when you know for sure that he or she is in the state that you want, even if it has not actually been prompted by you. Now calibrate that state when your meeting with your colleague is coming to a close. Is there a match between the characteristics of the state that you have noted elsewhere before and the one that you can see now? If yes, then you have been successful. If no, then you need to revisit what you are doing, and either do more or try something else.

## Spatial anchors

So far I have referred only to people and language as a source of anchoring. But we also use space in a similar way, and you can use this to help achieve your goals.

Imagine that you are doing a presentation in which you want to review the past and encourage the audience to think about the future. There are times in this presentation when you want to put forward your ideas without discussion. There are also times when you want to open up some of your thoughts for discussion. You can of course simply tell people how you want to do this, but you can make the message even more powerful by using space to signal your intentions.

You can decide which side of the room/platform you will use when you review the past. (The majority of people represent the past to their left, so, as you are facing the audience this will be to your right.) Each time you refer to the past, stand on this (ie your right) side of the room. When you refer to the future, walk across to the other side. There is no need for a  huge distance between the two as long as they are in clearly different places. If there is no room to walk from one side of the room to the other, you can still achieve the same effect by signalling to different sides with your hands as you refer to different time frames.

After doing this a few times, your position in the room or your hand-signals will already have created an expectation in your audience of whether you are going to refer to the past or the future when you speak. You have primed their unconscious minds to know what you will say next.

Remember the anchors that you have set up, and be sure to maintain them on future occasions.

## And finally...

The responsibility for the impression you create lies in the hands of one person alone – YOU.

# 7 do unto others

You may have already experimented with some of the ideas presented in this book. Maybe you have come into contact with NLP enthusiasts who are avidly learning and using everything they can lay their hands on! No matter what the level of enthusiasm, however, success depends on one important factor: your willingness to start with yourself.

If, for example, you have taken the skills of NLP and decided that you will use them as something with which to 'fix' other people – beware! This will not work. If you attempt to change others but do not change yourself, you will come unstuck.

### Case-study

Gandhi was famous for his counselling skills. One day, a mother brought her son to see him to ask his advice. When she was in his presence, she asked him if he could help. She explained that she wanted the Mahatma to stop her son eating sugar. Gandhi may have been surprised at the request, but he did not show it. Instead, he asked the mother to return in two weeks' time along with her son. She agreed and returned two weeks later. When she returned, Gandhi turned to the boy and said, 'Stop eating sugar.' The mother, with a look of surprise, turned to Gandhi and said, 'Thank you, but do you mind if I ask you a question?' Gandhi gestured to her to continue. 'Why did I have to go away and return after two weeks for you to give my son your advice?' Gandhi looked her directly in the eyes and replied, 'Two weeks ago I was eating sugar.'

In all my work using NLP to elicit what it is that makes the difference between models of best practice and what actually happens in the world, I would say that one factor stands head and shoulders above the rest:

*the ability and the willingness of individuals to be an example of the way that they would like to be treated themselves.*

## What are the telltale signs?

Have you ever had the feeling that something was not quite right when you were talking to someone, even though you just could not put your finger on what caused your unease? It is likely that your unconscious mind was picking up a discrepancy between what someone was saying and either what he or she was doing or the signals that he or she was giving non-verbally. We often sense these signals but sometimes push them to one side, believing that we should rely on 'objective' data alone. Even so, the unease will remain and will cloud your impression until you acknowledge what it is that bothers you. You yourself are always creating an impression on other people, even if it changes over time.

Chartered Institute of Personnel and Development

# Customer Satisfaction Survey

*We would be grateful if you could spend a few minutes answering these questions and return the postcard to CIPD. <u>Please use a black pen to answer</u>.* **If you would like to receive a free CIPD pen, please include your name and address.** IPD MEMBER Y/N

................................................................................................................................

1. Title of book ...........................................................................................................

2. Date of purchase:   month ................      year ...................

3. How did you acquire this book?
☐ Bookshop     ☐ Mail order     ☐ Exhibition   ☐ Gift      ☐ Bought from Author

4. If ordered by mail, how long did it take to arrive:
☐ 1 week      ☐ 2 weeks      ☐ more than 2 weeks

5. Name of shop ...............................  Town.......................................  Country ...........

6. Please grade the following according to their influence on your purchasing
   decision with 1 as least influential: (please tick)

|           | 1 | 2 | 3 | 4 | 5 |
|-----------|---|---|---|---|---|
| Title     |   |   |   |   |   |
| Publisher |   |   |   |   |   |
| Author    |   |   |   |   |   |
| Price     |   |   |   |   |   |
| Subject   |   |   |   |   |   |
| Cover     |   |   |   |   |   |

7. On a scale of 1 to 5 (with 1 as poor & 5 as excellent) please give your impressions
   of the book in terms of: (please tick)

|                     | 1 | 2 | 3 | 4 | 5 |
|---------------------|---|---|---|---|---|
| Cover design        |   |   |   |   |   |
| Paper/print quality |   |   |   |   |   |
| Good value for money|   |   |   |   |   |
| General level of service |   |   |   |   |   |

8. Did you find the book:

Covers the subject in sufficient depth     ☐ Yes        ☐ No
Useful for your work                       ☐ Yes        ☐ No

9. Are you using this book to help:
☐ In your work ☐ Personal study     ☐ Both     ☐ Other (please state)

*Please complete if you are using this as part of a course*

10. Name of academic institution.................................................................................

11. Name of course you are following? ........................................................................

12. Did you find this book relevant to the syllabus? ☐ Yes ☐ No    ☐ Don't know

**Thank you!**

To receive regular information about CIPD books and resources call 020 8263 3387.

21

**Publishing Department**

**Chartered Institute of Personnel and Development**

**CIPD House**

**Camp Road**

**Wimbledon**

**London**

**SW19 4BR**

Success in achieving your goals will depend both on how you manage this impression and on how it coincides with what you want it to be.

The most successful managers, leaders, salespeople, parents and friends are those who *are* an example of what they promote.

### Case-study

Aged 7, one of my sons once commented about his babysitter, 'Mrs Anderson said no, but her face was saying yes.' You might guess which signal was the more influential!

So just how can you co-ordinate the learning for both the conscious and the unconscious mind? Here are some pointers:

1   When you want to influence someone, decide what it is that you want that person to do, and how you want him or her to do it. Now ask yourself the question, 'How am I being an example of the behaviour that I would like from that person?'

2   What might be out of line for you, and what do you need
to do to be entirely congruent with your intentions and
your goals?

_____

_____

3   Which people do you recognise as being 'at one' with
themselves?

_____

_____

4   What kind of influence have these people had on you?

_____

_____

## Communicating with the unconscious as well as the conscious mind

Our unconscious mind is infinitely more powerful and
influential than our conscious mind, and yet we so often
overlook the ways that we can harness this resource in the
way we work. One of my goals in the way that I use NLP is
to make the unconscious conscious, and, in so doing, ensure
that I am giving messages that are aligned with both aspects
of my mind.

We are always communicating with people's unconscious minds. It is for this reason that we need to be aware of the way in which we are being an example of what we want. This is a question, as the next case-study shows, of being in rapport with ourselves.

### Case-study

Several years ago I was invited to do some training on sensitivity and rapport for some of the key personnel of a software house. The managing director was encouraged to attend by one of his senior managers, although there had been some doubt about his true feelings about this course. In the midst of some exercises concerned with enhancing the delegates' awareness of other people and their feelings, the MD took me to one side. Clearing his throat, he apologised and then said, 'You know, Sue, I'm just not a caring person!'

This incident highlighted for me the importance not only of paying attention to my instincts (I had suspected this might be his reaction) but also to knowing what needs to be addressed for there to be commitment at all levels. Let me illustrate this with a model, originally presented by Gregory Bateson, author of *Towards an Ecology of Mind*, and later developed by the international NLP trainer Robert Dilts.

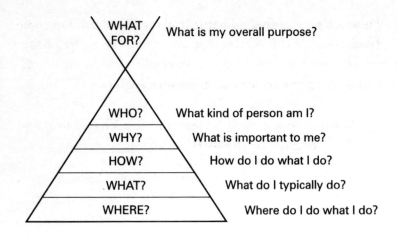

If all of these levels are aligned, then you are in a state of maximum influence. It is a state that athletes call the 'zone'. Everything you do feels right and you are at your most resourceful.

When did you last observe this state within yourself?

_____

_____

_____

If you do not have it now, what stops you from having it?

_____

_____

Here is a way to check what is true for you at each of these levels.

Consider the following questions for each level:

1   What is your overall purpose in life? What benefits do you seek to bring to others? (**Purpose**)

   ................................................................................................................

   ................................................................................................................

2   What kind of person are you, and how does this support the achievement of your overall purpose? (**Identity**)

   ................................................................................................................

   ................................................................................................................

3   What is important to you, and how does this support the kind of person you are? (**Values**)

   ................................................................................................................

   ................................................................................................................

4   How does what you believe support the achievement of what is important to you? (**Beliefs**)

   ................................................................................................................

   ................................................................................................................

5  What are your core talents, and how are you using them to achieve what is important to you? (**Capabilities**)

_____

_____

6  How is what you do (as a job and the way you behave moment by moment) an expression of who you truly are? (**Behaviour**)

_____

_____

7  How is your environment an expression of who you are, and how are the people around you supporting you in what you want? (**Environment**)

_____

_____

If all of these elements of yourself are pointing in the same direction, then you are _congruent_ ie everything about you says the same thing. This is a very influential state to have. The reactions that you get will be feedback to who you truly are.

## And finally...

*Example is the school of mankind, and they will learn at no other.*

Edmund Burke

# taking your learning further

There are many books on the use of NLP in different contexts available in most high-street bookstores. Do note, however, that what you get under the banner of NLP varies considerably depending on the author or the practitioner. I recommend you sample some texts first in order to find a style that suits you and your values.

## Other NLP books

KNIGHT S. *NLP at Work: The difference that makes the difference in business*. Nicholas Brealey Publishing.

A comprehensive explanation of the more popular applications of NLP in business.

KNIGHT S. *NLP Solutions: How to model what works in business and make it work for you*. Nicholas Brealey Publishing.

Explores how NLP can be used to make a real difference in business today, and explains the heart of NLP – the process of modelling.

KNIGHT S. *Personal Selling Skills: How NLP thinking can enhance your sales*. Burnham, Sue Knight Books & Talks.

A full-colour, A4 workbook that takes you through some of

the leading-edge ways of being successful in selling today.

LABORDE GENIE. Z. *Influencing with Integrity*. Syntony.

A beautifully illustrated explanation of NLP and influencing.

## Training in NLP

There are recognised levels of certification in NLP training. Some of the schools offering NLP certification are recognised by the Association for NLP (ANLP). Below is a list of the various levels of training.

| | |
|---|---|
| **Fundamentals of NLP (Personal Mastery):** | a foundation in the core principles |
| **Business Practitioner (Leadership for the Future):** | a recognised level of certification indicating that you can demonstrate to agreed standards the application of the core principles to yourself and to your coaching of others |
| **Master Practitioner (Pioneering Excellence):** | a recognised level of certification indicating that you are skilled in the core NLP techniques of modelling |
| **Trainer training:** | a recognised level of certification in your ability to |

train in NLP. This level of
certification means that you
are eligible to approve the
certification of others in the
skills of NLP.

With over 100,000 members, the **Chartered Institute of Personnel and Development** is the largest organisation in Europe dealing with the management and development of people. The CIPD operates its own publishing unit, producing books and research reports for human resource practitioners, students, and general managers charged with people-management responsibilities.

Currently there are over 160 titles covering the full range of personnel and development issues. The books have been commissioned from leading experts in the field and are packed with the latest information and guidance on best practice.

For free copies of the CIPD Books Catalogue, please contact the publishing department:

Tel.: 20-8263 3387
Fax: 020-8263 3850
E-mail: publish@cipd.co.uk/publications
Website: www.cipd.co.uk

Orders for books should be sent to:

Plymbridge Distributors
Estover
Plymouth
Devon
PL6 7PZ

(Credit card orders) Tel.: 01752 202 301
Fax: 01752 202 333

Other titles in the *Management Shapers* series:

## The Appraisal Discussion

Terry Gillen

Shows you how to make appraisal a productive and motivating experience for all levels of performer. It includes:

- assessing performance fairly and accurately

- using feedback to improve performance

- handling reluctant appraisees and avoiding bias

- agreeing future objectives

- identifying development needs.

1998  96 pages     0 85292 751 7

## Asking Questions

Ian MacKay

(Second Edition)

Will help you ask the 'right' questions, using the correct form to elicit a useful response. All managers need to hone their questioning skills, whether interviewing, appraising or simply exchanging ideas. This book offers guidance and helpful advice on:

- using various forms of open question – including probing, simple interrogative, opinion-seeking, hypothetical, extension and precision etc

- encouraging and drawing out speakers through supportive statements and interjections

- establishing specific facts through closed or 'direct' approaches

- avoiding counter-productive questions

- using questions in a training context.

1998  96 pages    0 85292 768 1

## Assertiveness

Terry Gillen

Will help you feel naturally confident, enjoy the respect of others and easily establish productive working relationships, even with 'awkward' people. It covers:

- understanding why you behave as you do and, when that behaviour is counter-productive, knowing what to do about it

- understanding other people better

- keeping your emotions under control

- preventing others' bullying, flattering or manipulating you

- acquiring easy-to-learn techniques that you can use immediately

- developing your personal assertiveness strategy.

1998  96 pages    0 85292 769 X

## Body Language at Work

Adrian Furnham

If we know how to send out the right body signals, we can open all sorts of doors for ourselves at work. If we get it wrong, those doors will be slammed in our faces. *Body Language at Work* explores how and why people communicate their attitudes, emotions and personalities in non-verbal ways.

The book examines:

- the nature and meaning of signals

- why some personalities are easy to read and others difficult

- what our appearance, clothes and mannerisms say about us

- how to detect office liars and fakes.

1999  96 pages     0 85292 771 1

## Conquer Your Stress

Cary L. Cooper and Stephen Palmer

In *Conquer Your Stress* two of the UK's most influential experts in stress management make clear it is frequently our misconceptions and ways of thinking that raise our stress levels. Conquering stress, they maintain, is no different from acquiring any other management skill – it just needs understanding and practice. With the help of self-assessment questionnaires and easy-to-follow activities, this perceptive book will enable you to:

● assess your own level and the stress-inducing ideas you hold

■ differentiate between negative signs of stress and positive ones of pressure

▲ reconsider your behaviour and health – with invaluable tips on time management, exercise, nutrition and relaxation methods

● avoid causing stress in others

● balance home and work priorities to become an effective 'life manager'.

2000  96 pages    0 85292 853 X

## Constructive Feedback

### Roland and Frances Bee

Practical advice on when to give feedback, how best to give it, and how to receive and use feedback yourself. It includes:

- using feedback in coaching, training, and team motivation
- distinguishing between criticism and feedback
- 10 tools of giving constructive feedback
- dealing with challenging situations and people.

1998  96 pages    0 85292 752 5

## The Disciplinary Interview

### Alan Fowler

This book will ensure that you adopt the correct procedures, conduct productive interviews and manage the outcome with confidence. It includes:

- understanding the legal implications
- investigating the facts and presenting the management case
- probing the employee's case and diffusing conflict
- distinguishing between conduct and competence
- weighing up the alternatives to dismissal.

1998  96 pages    0 85292 753 3

## Decision Making and Problem Solving

John Adair

*Decision Making and Problem Solving* explains the key principles for developing your thinking skills and applying them creatively and productively to every challenge. Acknowledged as an international authority on management thinking, Adair combines practical exercises with straightforward guidance on:

- ● understanding the way your mind works

- ■ adopting a structured approach to reach the best decision

- ▲ assessing risk and generating successful options for action

- ● using brainstorming and lateral thinking to increase your creativity

- ● creating a personal strategy to become a more effective practical thinker.

1999  96 pages      0 85292 807 6

## Effective Learning

### Alan Mumford

*Effective Learning* focuses on how we learn. It gives invaluable insights into ways in which you can develop your portfolio of skills and knowledge by managing and improving your ability to learn – positively and systematically. Practical exercises and clear guidance are given on:

- recognising the importance of 'achieved' learning
- understanding the learning process – the learning cycle and learning styles preferences
- taking best advantage of learning opportunities
- creating and implementing a personal development plan
- encouraging and managing a learning culture.

1999  96 pages  0 85292 777 0

## Getting a Better Job

John Courtis

Armed with *Getting a Better Job*, by one of the UK's top recruitment experts, you can be confident that a persuasive and polished interview will secure success. This book is an indispensable companion for all job-seekers, with lively tips and practical help on:

- finding your Unique Selling-Point

- writing a compelling CV and covering letter

- researching your targets and building up useful contacts

- ensuring an interview (even if there is no vacancy)

- taking discreet advantage of the interviewer to present yourself in the best possible light

- following up to make sure you clinch the job.

1999  96 pages    0 85292 806 8

## Leadership Skills

John Adair

*Leadership Skills* will give you confidence, guidance and inspiration as you journey from being an effective manager to becoming a leader of excellence. Acknowledged as a world authority on leadership, Adair offers stimulating insights on:

- recognising and developing your leadership qualities

- acquiring the personal authority to give positive direction and the flexibility to embrace change

- acting on the key interacting needs – to achieve your task, build your team and develop its members

- transforming such core leadership functions such as planning, communicating and motivating into practical skills that you can master.

1998 96 pages    0 85292 764 9

## Learning for Earning

Eric Parsloe and Caroline Allen

Today, lifelong learning is a must if you want to get onwards and upwards, and if you don't take charge of your own learning, then, frankly, no one else will. *Learning for Earning* shows exactly how to set about doing this.

The authors examine:

- using interactive exercises, quizzes and games to get you thinking

- how to reflect on what you have read and relate it to your own situation

- how to use other sources of information – people, organisations – to help you

- the use and benefits of 'action promises' – the actions you intend to take after reading.

1999  96 pages     0 85292 774 6

## Listening Skills

Ian MacKay
(Second Edition)

Improve your ability in this crucial management skill! Clear explanations will help you:

- recognise the inhibitors to listening

- listen to what is really being said by analysing and evaluating the message

- interpret tone of voice and non-verbal signals.

1998  80 pages    0 85292 754 1

## Making Meetings Work

Patrick Forsyth

Will maximise your time (both before and during meetings), clarify your aims, improve your own and others' performance and make the whole process rewarding and productive. The book is full of practical tips and advice on:

- drawing up objectives and setting realistic agendas

- deciding the who, where, and when to meet

- chairing effectively – encouraging discussion, creativity and sound decision-making

- sharpening your skills of observation, listening and questioning to get your points across

- dealing with problem participants

- handling the follow-up – turning decisions into action.

1998  96 pages     0 85292 765 7

## The Manager as Coach and Mentor

Eric Parsloe

(Second Edition)

*The Manager as Coach and Mentor* shows how and why coaching and mentoring provide the simplest, most practical and cost-effective ways of boosting the performance of your staff. It includes straightforward guidance on:

- choosing coaching styles and techniques that work

- understanding the roles and responsibilities of supportive mentoring

- developing the essential interpersonal skills and attributes

- assessing your own competence with simple exercises.

1999 96 pages    0 85292 803 3

# Managing for the First Time

Cherry Mill

Managing for the first time can seem like crossing a minefield but it should be exhilarating and satisfying! Based on the insights of 'first-timers' – younger and older – from all walks of business life, and from her own recent experience, Cherry Mill provides sound advice, encouragement and a few simple priorities so you can rise to the challenge with confidence and purpose. She covers:

- navigating your first 100 days – starting with impact and the critical things to get right for long-term success

- acting the part – learning the key management tasks and skills

- overcoming tricky situations – managing former peers, older or more experienced colleagues and those who seem to oppose you

- gaining credibility with your team and the respect of senior management

- focusing on things that make a difference and prioritising time – yours and others'

- seeking a mentor and establishing networks to give you support.

2000  96 pages     0 85292 858 0

## Motivating People

Iain Maitland

Will help you maximise individual and team skills to achieve personal, departmental and, above all, organisational goals. It provides practical insights into:

- becoming a better leader and co-ordinating winning teams

- identifying, setting and communicating achievable targets

- empowering others through simple job improvement techniques

- encouraging self-development, defining training needs and providing helpful assessment

- ensuring that pay and workplace conditions make a positive contribution to satisfaction and commitment.

1998  96 pages    0 85292 766 5

## Negotiating, Persuading and Influencing

Alan Fowler

Develop the skills you need to manage your staff effectively, bargain successfully with colleagues or deal tactfully with superiors. Sound advice on:

- probing and questioning techniques

- timing your tactics and using adjournments

- conceding and compromising to find common ground

- resisting manipulative ploys

- securing and implementing agreement.

1998  96 pages    ISBN 085292 755 X

## Persuasive Reports and Proposals

Andrew Leigh

*Persuasive Reports and Proposals* will ensure that what you write gets the results you want. It covers five crucial aspects which spell out PRIDE – what you should feel about your documents if they are to win hearts and minds:

● **P**urpose – clarifying your aim and constructing a persuasive argument

■ **R**eader – identifying and understanding your audience to anticipate objections and retain attention

▲ **I**mage – creating an appropriate style, tone and appearance while avoiding spoilers (poor spelling, grammar, literals etc) which undermine credibility

● **D**etail – using effective facts, sound structures, logical links and simple sentences

● **E**nhancers – seeking commitment, building in emotional appeal and editing to perfect your draft.

1999 96 pages     0 85292 809 2

## Working in Teams

Alison Hardingham

Looks at teamworking from the inside. It will give you valuable insights into how you can make a more positive and effective contribution – as team member or team leader – to ensure that your team works together and achieves together. Clear and practical guidelines are given on:

- understanding the nature and make-up of teams

- finding out if your team is on track

- overcoming the most common teamworking problems

- recognising your own strengths and weaknesses as a team member

- giving teams the tools, techniques and organisational support they need.

1998  96 pages    0 85292 767 3